The Book of Butterflies

Dr. Diana Prince

AuthorHouse™
1663 Liberty Drive
Bloomington, IN 47403
www.authorhouse.com
Phone: 1 (800) 839-8640

Published by AuthorHouse 06/21/2019

ISBN: 978-1-7283-1672-7 (sc)
ISBN: 978-1-7283-1673-4 (hc)
ISBN: 978-1-7283-1671-0 (e)

Library of Congress Control Number: 9781728316710

Print information available on the last page.

PHOTOS: All photographs are used with permission of Getty Images.

This book is printed on acid-free paper.

authorHOUSE®

Contents

List of Photos

Introduction

The Butterfly is among the most beautiful of nature's creatures. There are thousands of butterfly species in the world, each with its distinct markings and splendid colors.

Many ancient cultures believed that the butterfly represented the human soul set free. Today, butterflies continue to astound us with their beauty and their brilliance.

The World of Butterflies

There are over 20,000 species of butterflies in the world. They have an astonishing variety of shapes and they are known worldwide for their magnificent array of colors.

Butterflies are very versatile and adaptable. They have been able to adapt to altitudes in the world's highest mountain ranges. They are also able to adapt to dry and very tropical climates. They exist on every continent, with the exception of the ice-bound continent of Antarctica.

Butterflies originated in the Mesozoic Era which is a period that lasted 65 to 145 million years ago. In some ancient Cretaceous rock, the impressions of early butterflies can be seen in the outlines or shapes preserved in rock, although their fragile physical bodies did not survive.

A scientist who studies the life, development and habits of butterflies is known as a "Lepidopterist".

In some cultures and traditions, butterflies are believed to represent the souls of departed loved ones. They also represent a transformation from a physical to a spiritual life, when compared to their process of metamorphosis from a caterpillar to a radiant, transformed butterfly.

The word for butterfly in Russia is "babochka", which translates to "tiny soul". The Greek work "psyche" is also used to refer to butterflies. Psyche was the goddess who represented the soul. In art she is depicted with butterfly wings.

While butterflies have a sense of touch, they cannot feel pain. This is because their brain and nervous systems do not have pain receptors.

Butterflies and Moths

Both butterflies and moths belong to the insect order called "Lepidoptera", a word derived from the Greek word "ptera", which means "wing".

In this insect group there are over 165,000 different species. While both moths and butterflies fall into this group, the number of moth species far outweighs the butterflies. Moth species make up about 145,000 of these types, while the remaining species of butterflies number about 20,000 specific types.

Many observers, used to the more common white or brown moths ordinarily seen, conclude that only butterflies can lay claim to the brilliant colors that we usually associate with them. This is a great misconception, since some moths, especially in some tropical locations, can sometimes rival even the most stunning hues of butterflies.

Their main similarity is that during their metamorphosis, they both pass through the same developmental stages. They both experience evolving from egg, to caterpillar, to chrysalis and finally emerging in their adult stage fully formed.

They also have some clear differences. For instance, the antennae of the butterfly is usually extended outward and forward, and ends in small black knobs at the end. In moths, there is no knob at the end of their antennae. The antenna of the moth is generally shorter than the butterfly, and it has a small feathering-type ending when seen under a microscope.

Also, butterflies tend to be slimmer, while moths have thicker bodies, and sometimes fuzzy bodies, which are very rare for butterflies.

Their living habits also vary. Butterflies are active during the day, while moths are nocturnal and active at night.

Size

With thousands of butterfly species, the size variations are endless. However, the largest butterfly in the world is believed to be the butterfly known as *"Queen Alexandra's Birdwing"*. This is a species only found in New Guinea. It occupies the vast rainforests. The span of the wings can measure a foot in length from wing tip to wing tip.

The female of this species is larger than the male, specifically two inches greater in the diameter of her wings.

The next largest butterfly is the *"Old World Swallowtail"*, also known as the *"African Giant Swallowtail Birdwing"*, in which the adult butterfly will have an average wingspan of ten inches.

There may be even larger butterflies in some of the remote regions of the world. Peru, for example, has almost 4,000 different species of butterflies. These inhabit some of the most remote and inaccessible places. The butterfly species in Peru are believed to account for nearly 22 percent of the butterfly species in the world.

The *"Blue Pygmy"* butterfly is considered the smallest of the world's butterflies. It is native to Southern California and other parts of the American southwest. This small butterfly measures only half an inch from wing tip to wing tip.

The heart of the butterfly is long and slender, and it is located on the upper side of its body. It extends the length of its body.

Relative to size and growth, an interesting fact is that after a *Monarch* butterfly emerges from its chrysalis as an adult, it ceases to grow any further.

Wings

The many different species of butterflies have tiny translucent scales. They overlay each other in dense rows, and their compact alignment often produces shiny, smooth iridescent colors.

The wings can provide an effective camouflage and protect and hide the butterflies in plain sight. However, in some rare cases, butterflies are protected by a "lack of coloration", which can protect them from predators by making them seem invisible. In these rare instances, they sometimes have almost no coloration in their wings, and the wings appear, instead, as a transparent membrane. When observed from above, they seem to disappear altogether when resting among the plants or flowers. An example of this is the butterfly known as the "Glasswing", in which the transparent wings make the insect almost invisible to the eye of predators.

Another interesting protective feature of the wings, is the markings on the wings sometimes known as "eyespots". Dark concentric designs on the wings can make them look like "eyes" are peering out of the wing. This can confuse predators into thinking these black concentric spots are the eyes of other animals looking out at them, and posing a potential threat.

Also, some predators will avoid butterflies with bright orange markings, such as the monarch butterfly, or other butterflies with similar colored wings. This is because such butterflies frequently consume toxins which, while safe for the butterflies, are intolerable to predators. This can make these butterflies taste very bitter, and this causes predators to avoid them.

Another important function of the wings of the butterfly is the role that they play during the mating ritual in attracting and finding a mate.

Diet

Butterflies extract their nourishment from the nectar of flowers. In return, the plants rely on butterflies for pollination, and their own continued propagation – depending on the butterflies to carry their plant seeds elsewhere in the process.

The butterfly drinks nectar from flowers using its long nose-like feature called a "proboscis."

Butterflies do not have mouths, so their nourishment is restricted to the nectar obtained and ingested through the proboscis.

But even more remarkable is that butterflies have the ability to taste with their feet. Their feet are equipped with small tubes which suction what they ingest. This nourishment then passes into their systems.

Flowers are not the only sources of food for butterflies. They will sometimes scavenge for different organic matter such as tree sap or dead animals in addition to the various plants, leaves and seeds that are readily accessible. Some butterflies will also eat small bugs. Fruits in a state of decay may also be ingested.

Butterflies are the object of a number of other predators. They are eaten by reptiles, birds and other insects.

Butterflies can sometimes ingest toxins from certain plants, which will not harm them, but which will repel or kill other animals. For example, **Monarch** butterflies can ingest complex enzymes from plants which will make them taste bitter to their predators. Such predators will avoid certain wing patterns, particularly bright orange markings on the wings, which identify butterflies who regularly consume such toxins. These toxins can kill or make their predators sick if they eat these butterflies.

Vision

Butterflies have the unusual ability to see ultra violet light. They also have about 5,800 lenses in their eyes which make them adept at seeing the smallest of movements. Their keen vision also protects them from lurking predators. Since humans cannot see in the ultra violet range, it is believed that there may be some features that butterflies can see that humans cannot. There could be, for instance, light ranges of an ultraviolet nature which we cannot decipher, since humans are unable to process ultraviolet light.

While butterflies predominantly see green, yellow and red, they are unable to recognize many other colors.

Butterflies have two sets of eyes. The first set of eyes is called the "simple eyes" or "ocelli". This kind of eye detects the brightness of the surrounding light sources. They cannot focus on individual objects.

The second set of eyes has a different purpose. These are called "compound eyes", and they primarily focus on details. They are more versatile than the ocelli. These compound eyes, while not having a great range of color, *do* give the butterfly a 360-degree range of vision. The compound eyes provide excellent peripheral vision.

The eyes of the butterfly are continuously open, because they have no eyelids.

Camouflage

Camouflage is an important element of protection for some butterflies. Some butterfly species which are brilliantly colored may escape detection from predators by hiding among bright flowers or blooms of similar color.

Others may blend in with tree bark or other textures in which their colors will be less obvious against the background.

The astonishing variations of colors found among butterflies makes this possible.

The texture and patterns of the wings often mimic the natural environment or surrounding surfaces. These may be patterns that mimic rocky surfaces or surrounding plants against which the butterfly is so "blended", that the butterfly seems to "disappear in plain sight."

This is not the only case in which animals benefit from "hiding" from predators. However, butterflies have an astonishing array of ways to accomplish this. Because of their infinite variety of forms and markings, the butterflies have a dazzling ability to effectively conceal themselves in their surroundings. The wings are the primary means of effecting this protective mechanism. Some markings or designs on their wings resemble the leaves or flowers in which the butterflies often rest.

The "Indian Oakleaf" butterfly can fold its wings closed, and appear to be a dried, dead leaf. In some rare cases, certain species of butterflies have few pigments in their wings, and they can appear almost transparent and clear to predators who literally "see through" the wings, as the insects rest on plants and flowers.

In some cases, certain butterfly species have toxins in their body which smell and repel their predators.

Mating

The mating process is an elaborate series of steps. First, the male butterfly selects one of his own species to "court". He then tries to attract her attention by circling upward in the sky, in a ritual kind of dance, meant to attract the female butterfly's interest. The male then circles down to the ground, continuing the dance. During this time, as he attempts to get the attention of the female, he shows aggression toward any other males nearby.

In the next step, he will face and approach the female, and hold her as their abdomens touch, and he deposits his sperm in the female. She retains the sperm, and the eggs are later fertilized as they leave her body.

During this process the male emits pheromones. These are scents or smells which attract the females. They are produced in black pouches in the males. During the mating, these scents are emitted and attract the attention of the females.

During their lives, the males will mate several times, but usually the female will only mate once in her life. During the mating, after the sperm is used to fertilize the eggs, they will stay in the female body over time. The female will later deposit the eggs on plants. One of the most common plants the female chooses, when she is ready to deposit the eggs, is the milkweed plant. Over her lifetime, the female will lay about 100 eggs.

After the offspring emerges from the pupa as a brilliant butterfly, the new butterfly is an "adult", and is capable of mating within an hour of his birth.

Metamorphosis

The metamorphosis of the butterfly, which leads to the final adult butterfly, goes through four specific life stages. The word "metamorphosis" means "change". Each stage of development brings a specific series of physical changes.

First, the female, after mating, lays her eggs on a plant. When the egg hatches, the plant is eaten by the newly emerged caterpillar.

Second, the caterpillar continues to consume nourishment, and sheds additional skin which results from the insect's quickly growing body.

Thirdly, the caterpillar, will wrap himself in silk-like threads that suspend him from a nearby branch or twigs. Often this will harden into a husk-shaped and protective shell. The small confined capsule in which the developing butterfly lives during this period is called the chrysalis, and it is also referred to as a "pupa" or "larva". During this time the internal structures develop.

Fourth, after a period, usually of a few days, the adult butterfly disengages himself from the confinement of the pupa, and emerges as a fully developed adult.

The transformation through the process of the four stages of metamorphosis shows the distinct sequence which occurs in the development of the butterfly. The time each successive stage takes place may sometimes vary depending on the type of butterfly involved.

The following pages look at these four specific stages. These are the **Egg Stage**, the **Caterpillar Stage**, the **Chrysalis Stage** and the **Butterfly Stage**.

Egg Stage

STAGE 1

After the mating of the male and the female, the fertilized egg is deposited in the female. She then lays the egg on the leaves of a plant, which is called a "host plant". The most preferred plant for this purpose is the milkweed, which provides the best nutrients for the growth and development of the eggs. This usually takes place in March or April.

(5 to 10 days in duration)

Caterpillar Stage

STAGE 2

The "Caterpillar Stage" is also known as the "Larva Stage". At this time, the newly formed caterpillar emerges from the egg which the mother had deposited on a plant. This caterpillar begins to devour the plant on which the egg had been laid. This growth stage of the caterpillar is characterized by continual eating. The great amount of food devoured during this time, stretches his skin and causes it to shed. Up to eight layers of external skin are sloughed off in this process, which is called "molting".

(10 to 14 days in duration)

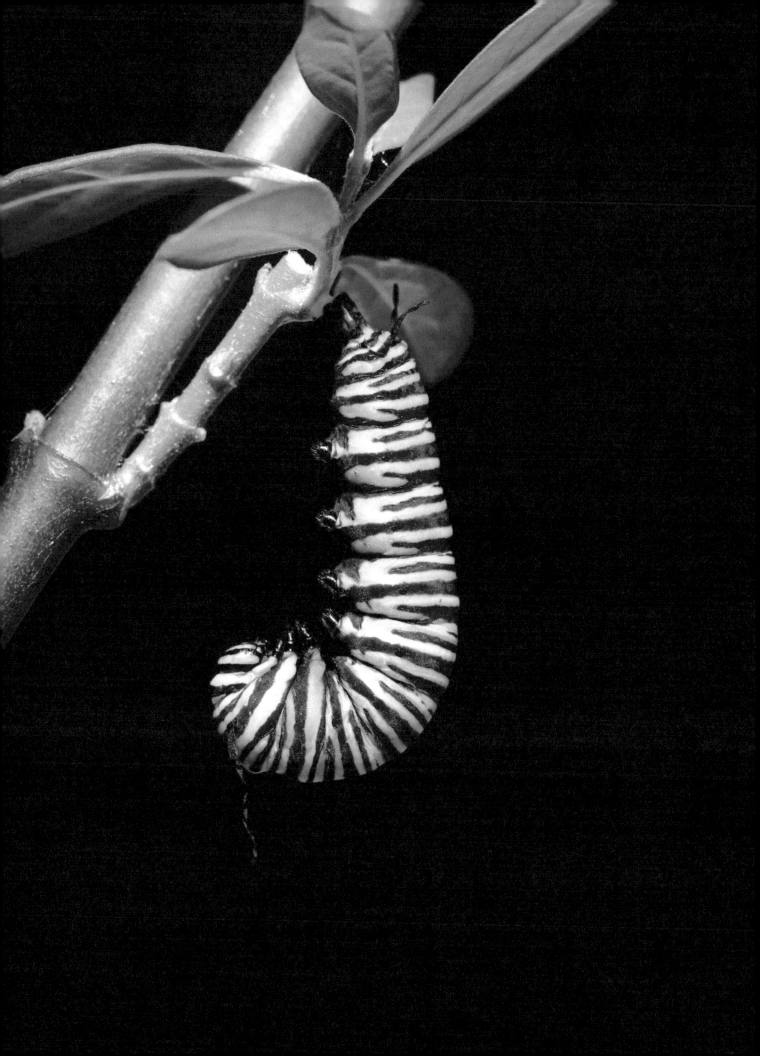

Chrysalis Stage

STAGE 3

The Chrysalis is the third stage of development. The Chrysalis is the silken structure in which the developing insect is encased. This outer casing hardens around the developing butterfly, and it is also referred to as the "pupa" or "cocoon".

Unlike the often colorful butterfly which will eventually emerge from the chrysalis, this living "container" for the developing butterfly may be clear, or a shade of brown in color. Inside new tissue forms. The "pupa" protects the butterfly as the new life inside grows and develops.

(10 to 16 days in duration)

Butterfly Stage

STAGE 4

Eventually, the fully formed butterfly emerges from the chrysalis, and this completes the cycle. However, the stage during which the butterfly is encased within the pupa can vary greatly. This "gestation" or resting period during which the pupa protects the developing adult butterfly, will normally take only a few days. However, in some rare cases, certain species may take a year for this final process to complete itself.

Adult Butterfly Emerges

Life Span

Surprisingly, butterflies live a relatively short life span. Some live only a few short days after exiting from their pupa, and first spreading their wings. The average life span, however, depending on the type of butterfly, is generally about 30 days. A smaller number of butterflies, and normally an exception, are some species which survive between five and seven months.

It is interesting that butterflies in the larva stage as caterpillars often live longer in that form than they do as adult butterflies.

The respective stages of development from egg to caterpillar, and then from chrysalis to adult, are somewhat similar from one species of butterfly to another. However, the length of time they live after emerging as adult butterflies, can vary considerably. Females tend to outlive male butterflies by about five days on average.

The longest living butterflies can generally live eight months to a year. The Monarch butterfly has one of the longest life spans, and can live up to eleven months. The Mourning Cloak butterflies also have long lives with an average lifespan of a year.

For some butterflies, two-weeks is an average life span. Some noted exceptions exist, particularly in tropical climates, where butterflies may live only 2 to 5 days on average after reaching adult hood.

The length of the butterfly's life is also related to their mating cycles, and their reproduction over their lifetimes. For example, the males die about eight weeks after using all of their sperm mating with different females. The female butterfly, however, lives until she has laid all of her eggs.

Annual Migration

Depending on climate and other external factors, several species of butterflies are known to migrate. While much is known about the lengthy migration of the Monarchs, very little is known about other species of butterflies.

For one thing, not all butterflies migrate every year. For instance, many butterflies in Florida, a moderate and warm climate, remain year round.

Many butterflies, with the exception of the Monarch butterfly, will usually endure the winter in either the caterpillar or chrysalis state. The Monarch butterflies have the least tolerance for cold, which is why they are willing to travel great distances over thousands of miles, to avoid it.

Other butterflies will hibernate in shelters such as holes in trees during the winter, and do not abandon their established locales. Some will find houses or sheds with protection against the cold. Others may move to nearby locations closer to home where they can find a place most conducive to weathering winter cold. These closer options will rarely involve travelling great distances like the monarchs.

For most species, the winter hideaway can be relatively close to their year round homes. They tend to follow specific directional patterns to their nearby winter homes. For instance, *Mourning Cloak* butterflies, *Queen* Butterflies and *Cloudless Sulphurs* will usually fly in a southerly course to find the nearest shelter from the cold. Others, such as the *Common Buckeye,* the *Fiery Skipper,* the *Red Admiral* and the *Painted Lady* butterflies, will head in a northerly trajectory to find the nearest relief from inclement weather.

Monarch Butterfly Migration

The monarch butterfly migration is hailed as one of the most spectacular events among butterfly enthusiasts. Within the cycles of migration, the Monarch Butterfly is particularly interesting. Unlike most other butterflies who migrate into nearby territory, the monarchs will often travel thousands of miles during their migration. Early monarch migrations were mentioned in the folklore of ancient Indian tribes. Often the colorful arrival of the species signaled the beginning of the corn harvest.

During their two-month migration period, the Monarch Butterflies travel over 2,000 miles. Their course takes them from Canada and the northern states to as far south as Mexico and as far west as California.

The earliest scientific studies of monarch migrations date to the 1930's and the work of a Canadian researcher, Fred Urquhart. He studied the destinations of monarch populations to determine movement of the monarchs in their annual migrations. He tagged thousands of the butterflies in an effort to determine their routes and favorite sites.

The Monarch Butterfly Biosphere Reserve near Mexico City is known to be a primary gathering site for monarch populations migrating from east of the Rocky Mountains. They congregate in the forested habitats of cedar, pine and oak. These rural colonies can exceed 80 million butterflies.

Other monarch butterfly populations congregate in Florida, and these stay year-round and do not migrate.

It has been noted that in some migrating colonies, the monarchs often have dwindling numbers of females, and scientists are not in consensus about the cause of their declining numbers.

About the Author

Diana Prince has a Master's Degree in English and a Master's Degree in Philosophy from California State University at San Diego. She also has a PhD. in Psychology from United States International University.

Printed in the United States
By Bookmasters